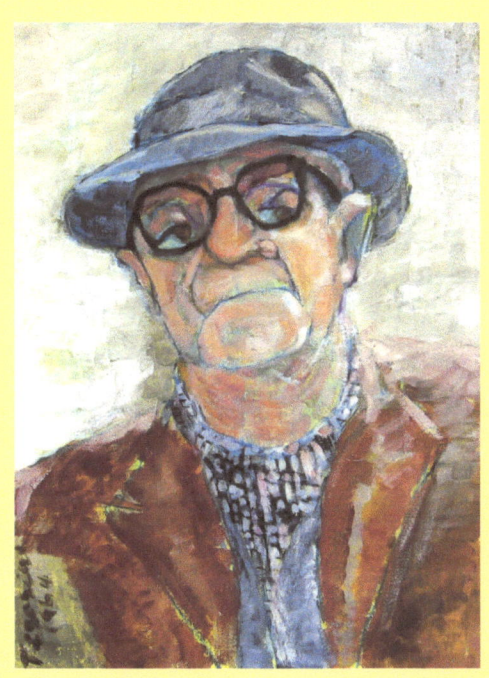

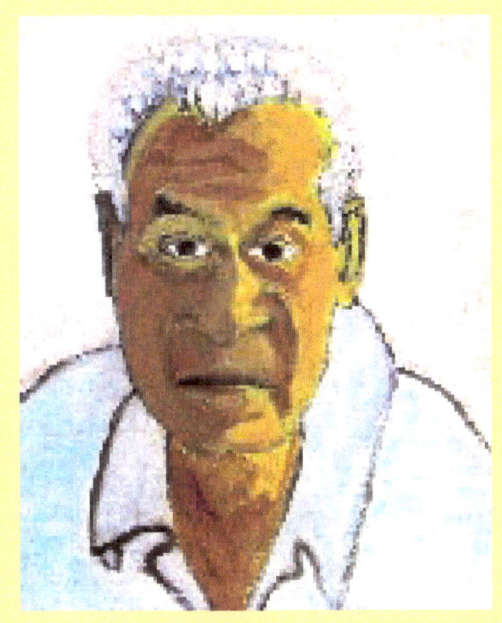

Ugo and His Pictures
The Story of Ugo Tesoriere

by Cecilia Cerasoli

Photographs of the work of Ugo Tesoriere from the Tesoriere
Collection are used with the permission of Mepkin Abbey,
Moncks Corner, South Carolina

Book Design by Genevieve Cerasoli
Copyright © 2011 Cecilia Cerasoli
All Rights Reserved

ISBN -13:978-1461066026
ISBN-10: 1461066026
LLCN: 2011905657
Printed in South Carolina, USA

An artist

*is a man, woman or child who **observes***

the world around them, and expresses what

they think about it by making pictures or sculpture,

writing stories or music, playing musical instruments,

dancing or acting.

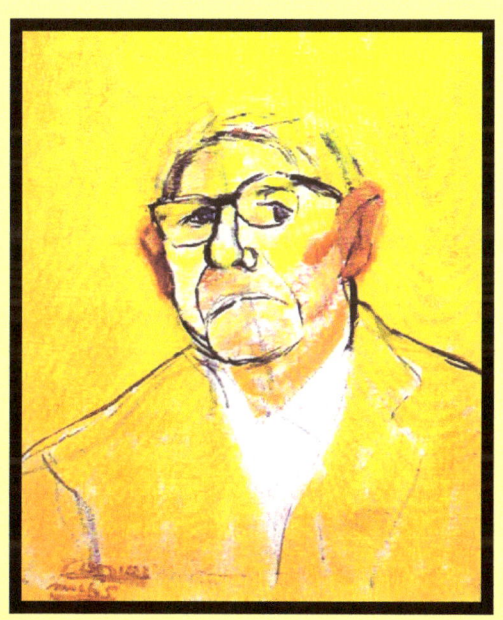

DEDICATION

To Ugo Tesoriere,

who taught me what it means to be a real artist;

To Valeria Giannini,

his wife, muse and vigilant supporter;

...and to my dear friend Francis,

who introduced me to Ugo and his pictures.

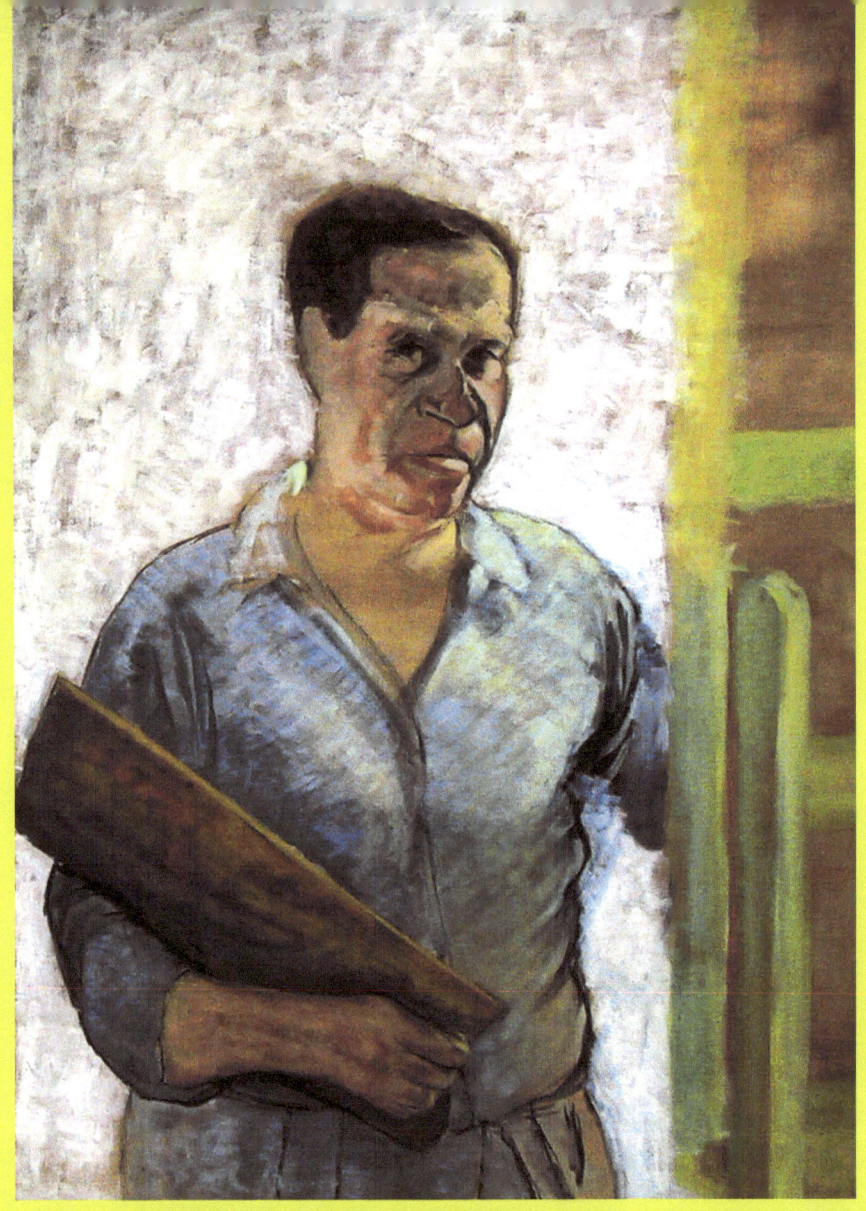

I want to tell you a story about a visual artist who expressed his feelings about the world around him by making pictures.

His name is **Ugo Tesoriere**.

Did you ever meet an artist?
Can anyone be an artist?

Ugo's Mom and Dad were born in Italy. Their names were Ambrosina and Antonio. Many years ago, Ugo's parents decided to move to the United States. They chose to live in Brooklyn, New York , where Ugo and his brothers were born. When he grew up, Ugo studied hard and became a doctor. He worked in a hospital in New York and helped many people get well.

Throughout his life, Ugo loved to read books. He also loved to look at pictures made by artists. For many years, he collected art, but eventually decided to be an artist himself and make his own pictures.

What do **you** really love to do?

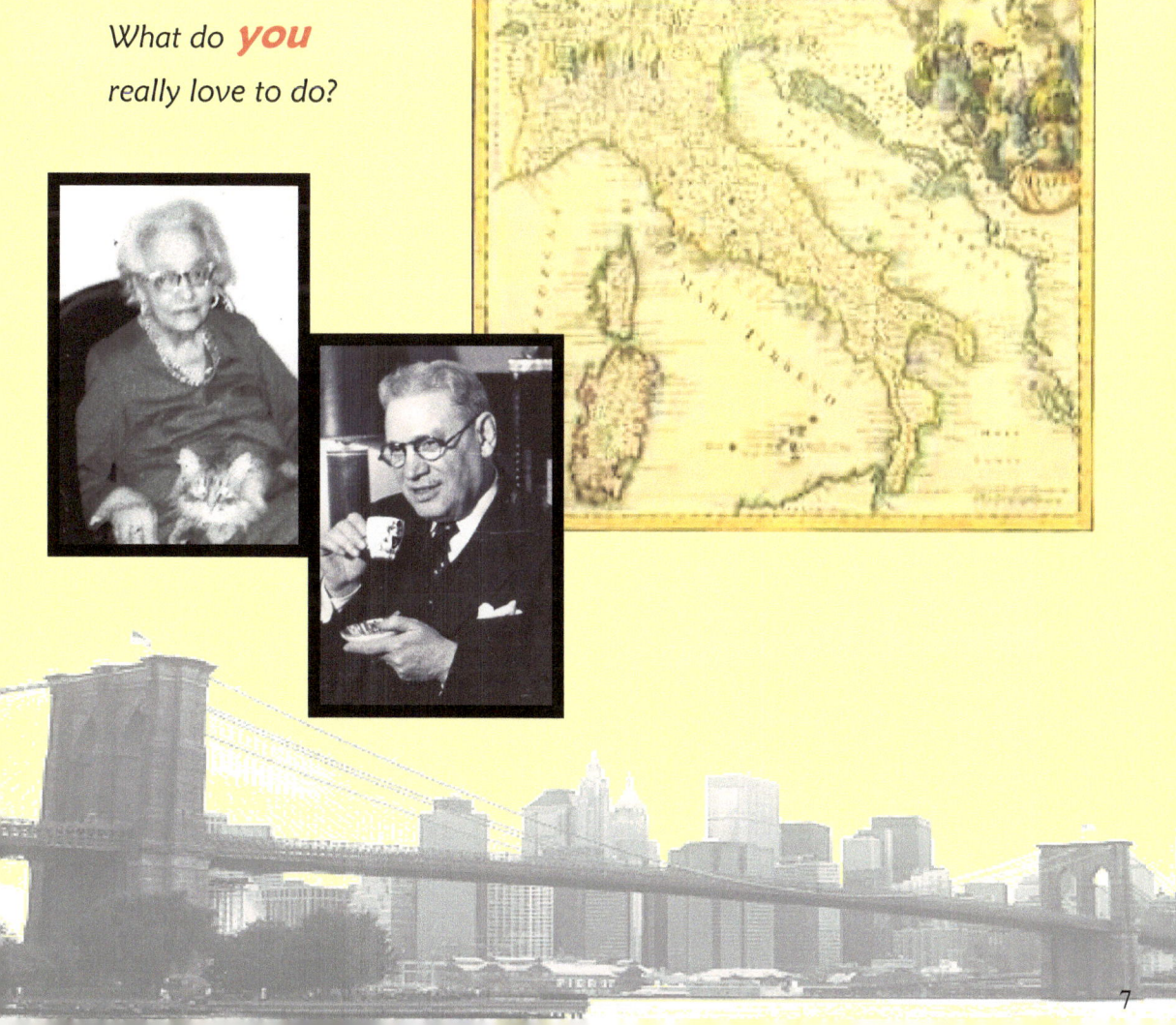

Many famous artists have lived in Italy, so Ugo decided
to go to Italy, his family's homeland, to learn about art
and to make his pictures.

Two famous artists from Italy are Leonardo Da Vinci
and Michelangelo Buonarroti. This is what they looked like.

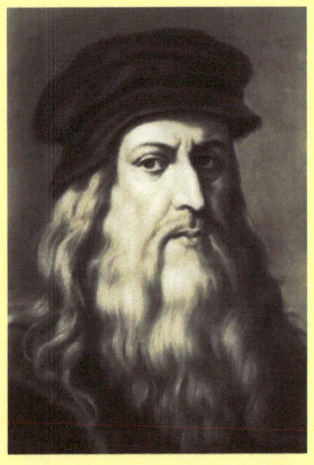

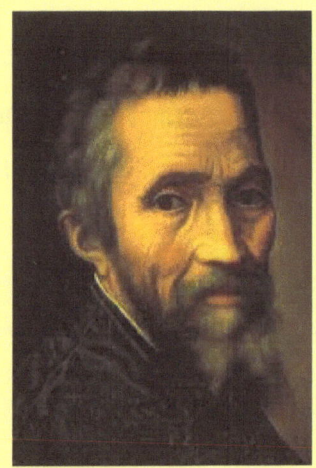

Leonardo Da Vinci
(1452-1519)

Michelangelo Buonarroti
(1475-1564)

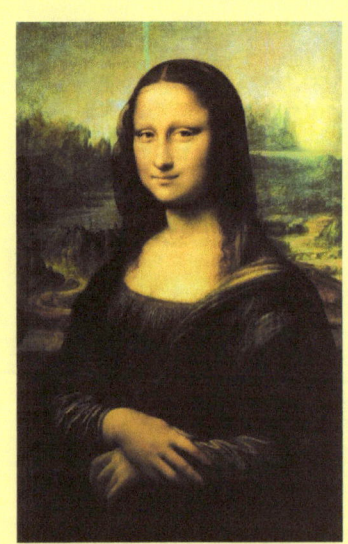

Leonardo Da Vinci made a very
famous picture of a lady. Leonardo called
his picture La Gioconda, which means
"The Happy Lady" but most people call
her Mona Lisa. What do you think Mona
was happy about?

Most people don't know that
Leonardo painted this picture on a piece
of wood. Most paintings are painted on
fabric called canvas.

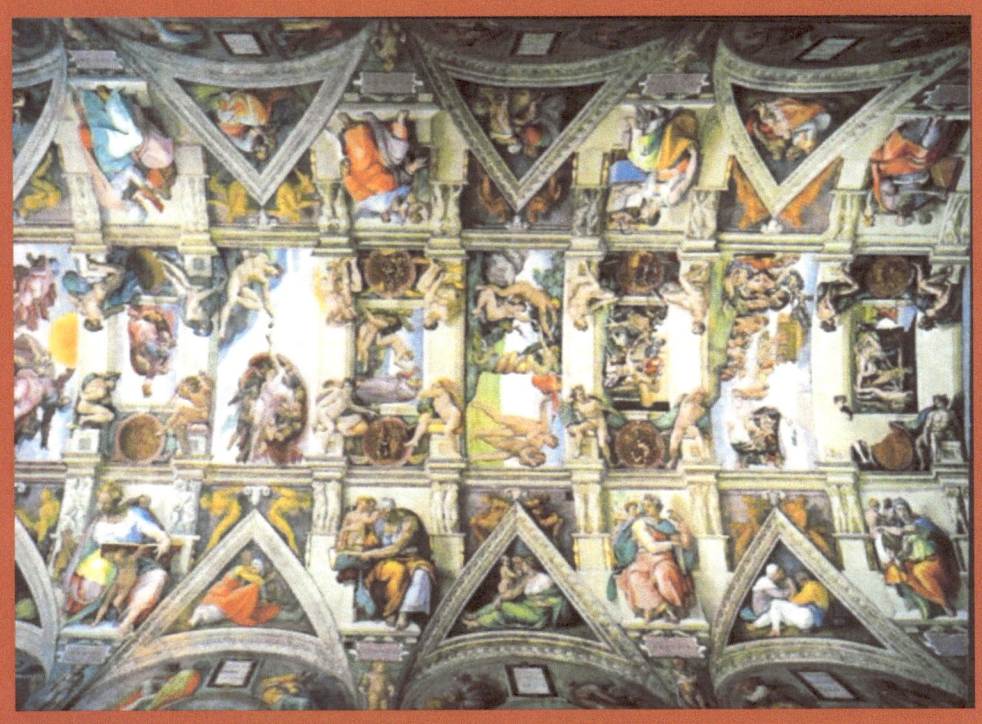

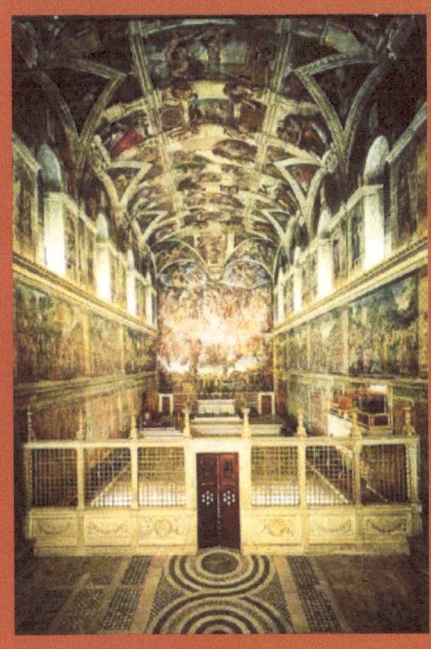

Michelangelo painted pictures on the huge ceiling of a room, called the **Sistine Chapel** in Rome. These pictures told stories from the bible.

Do you know any stories?

Have you ever drawn pictures of them?

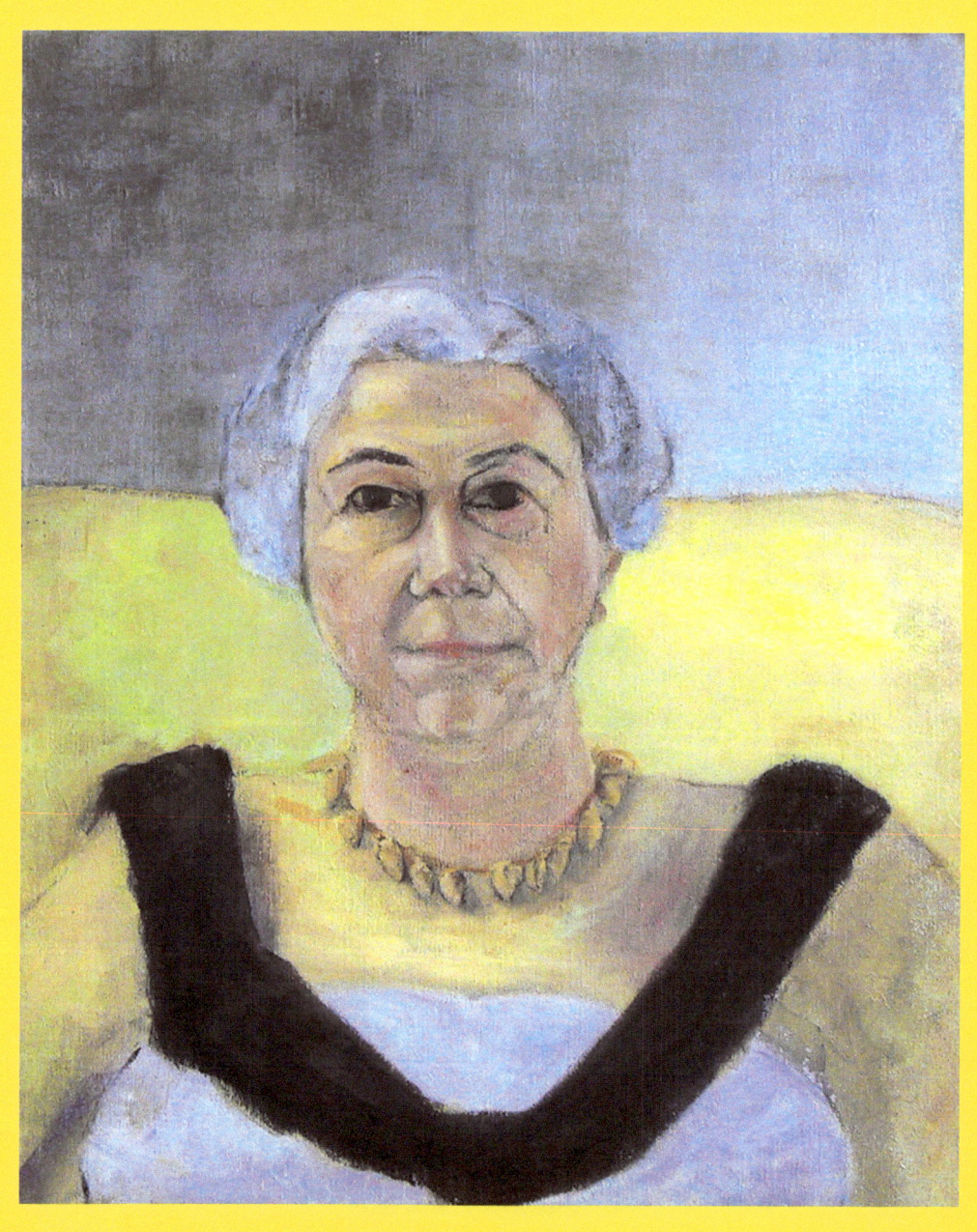

This is Valeria.

When Ugo went to Italy, he went to a famous school for artists called **L' Accademia di Belle Arti,** which means " the school of beautiful art."

He married a lady named **Valeria**, and they lived together for 40 years. They lived on a street in Rome called the Via Giulia, where artists lived many years ago.
It is very possible that Michelangelo lived there too when he was painting his famous ceiling.

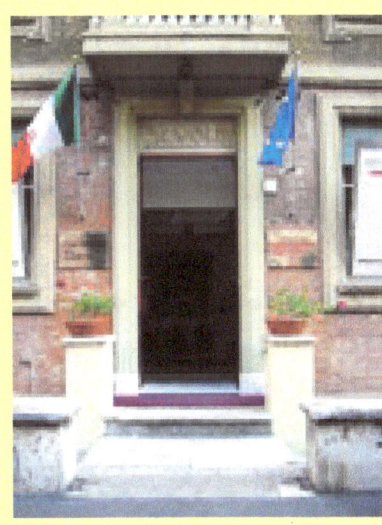

L'Accademia Belle Arti,
Ugo's school in Rome

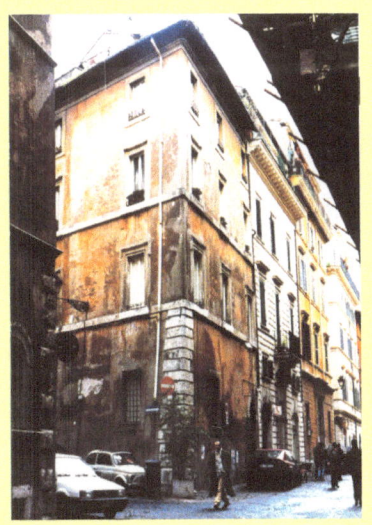

This is the house
where Ugo and Valeria lived.
Via Giulia, 83, Rome

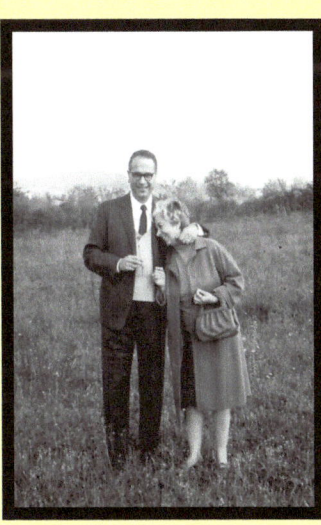

Ugo and Valeria
on their land in the country

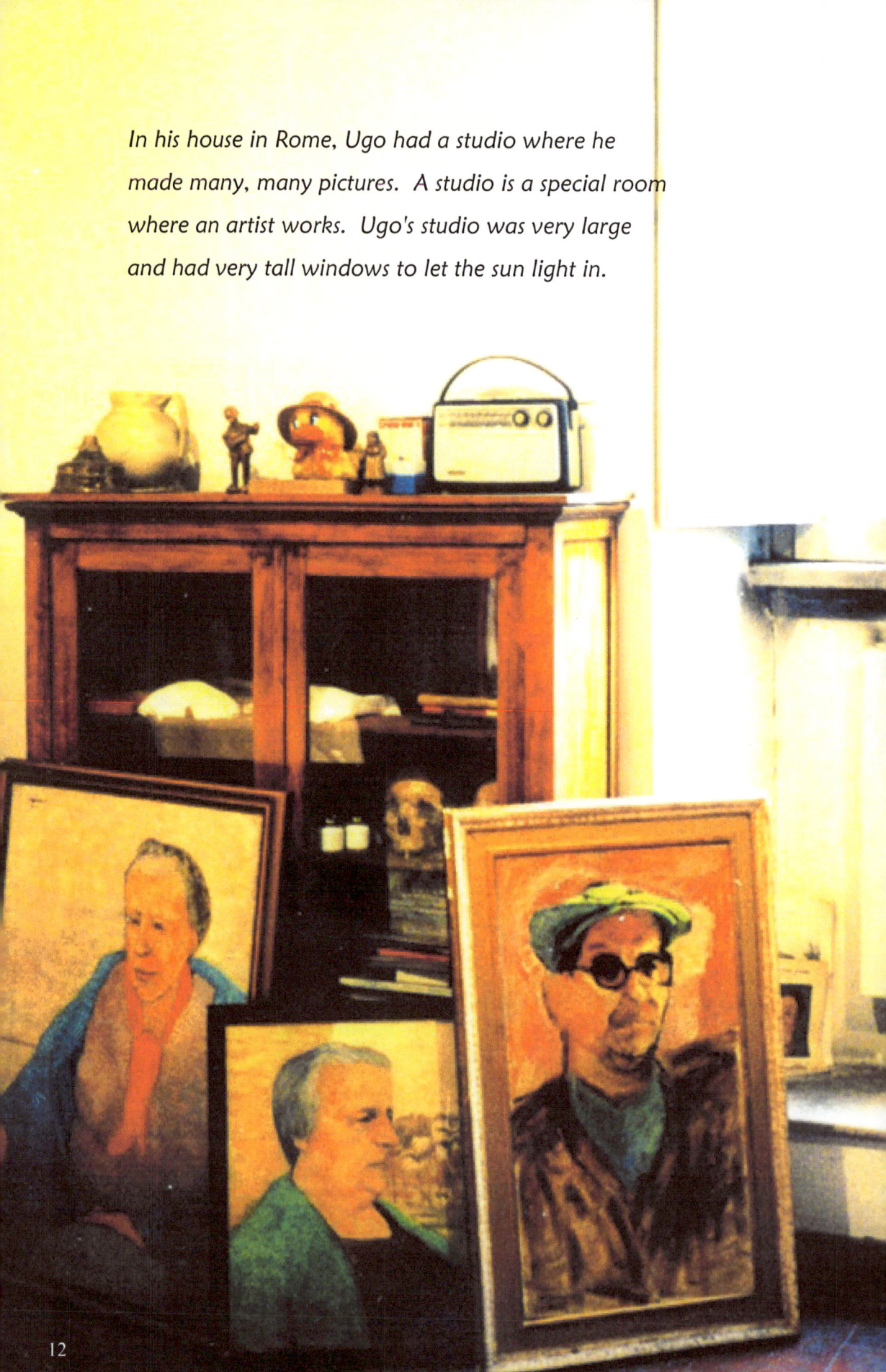

In his house in Rome, Ugo had a studio where he made many, many pictures. A studio is a special room where an artist works. Ugo's studio was very large and had very tall windows to let the sun light in.

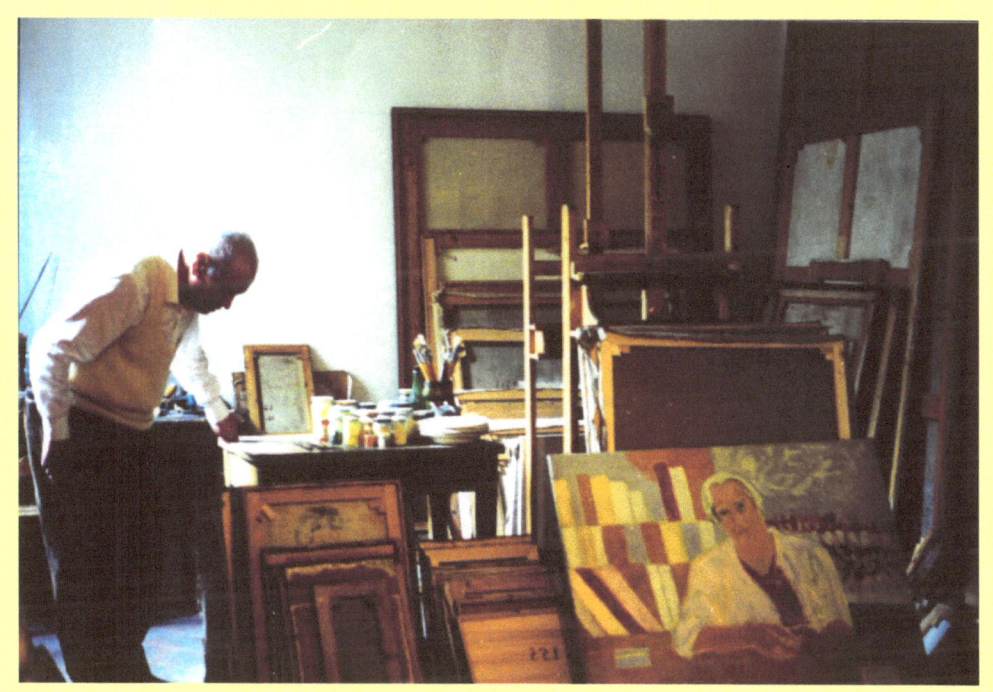

Why is it important to have lots of light in an artist's studio?

Do you have a special place to do your work?

Can you guess how many pictures Ugo made?

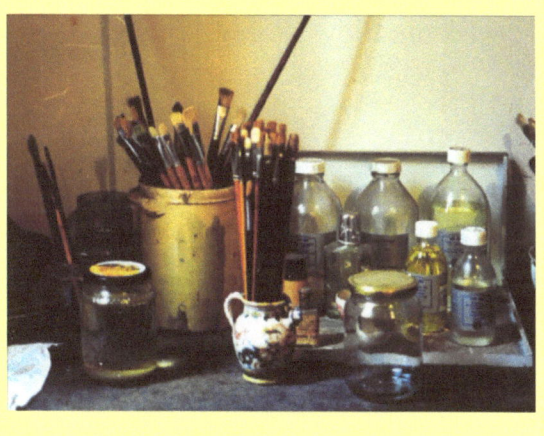

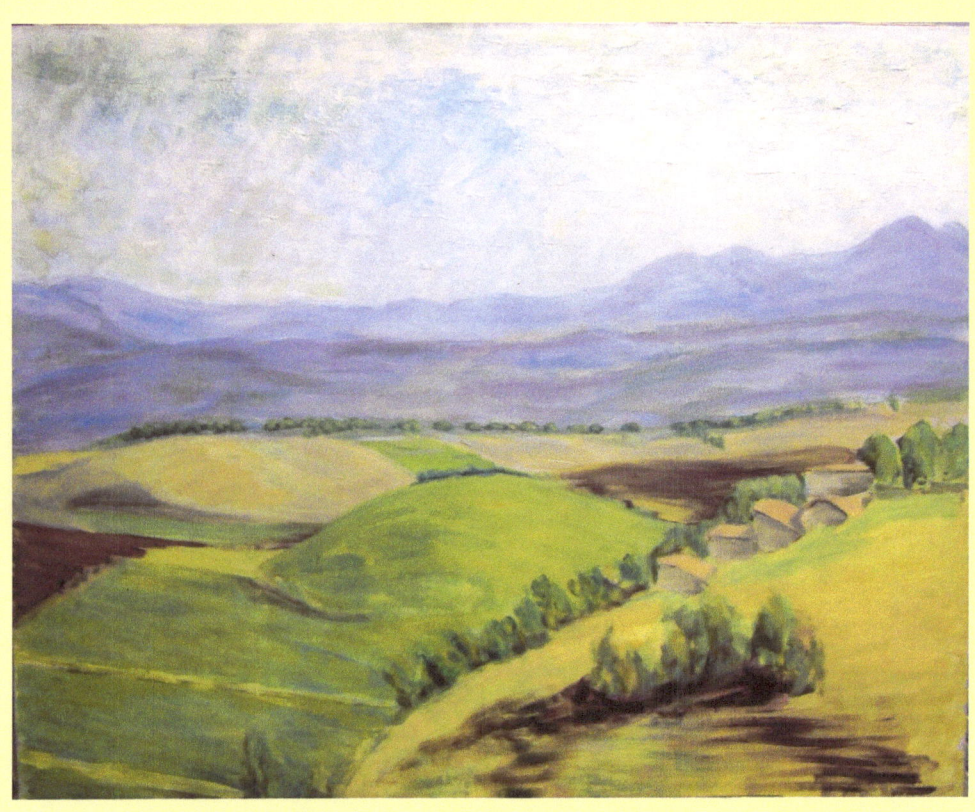

Ugo made over 1000 pictures!

He made many different types of pictures using pencils, chalk, ink, and paint.

Some show people,
some show things
and some show places.

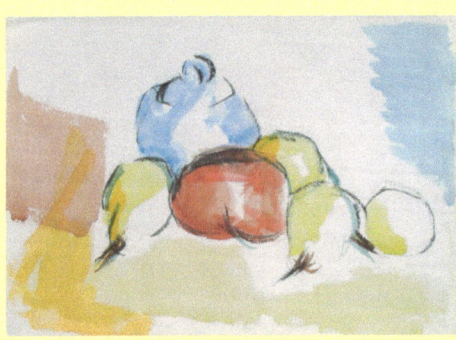

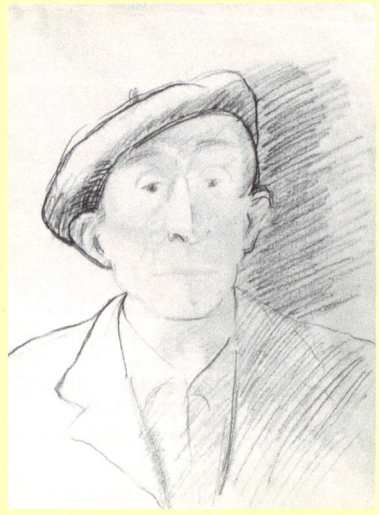

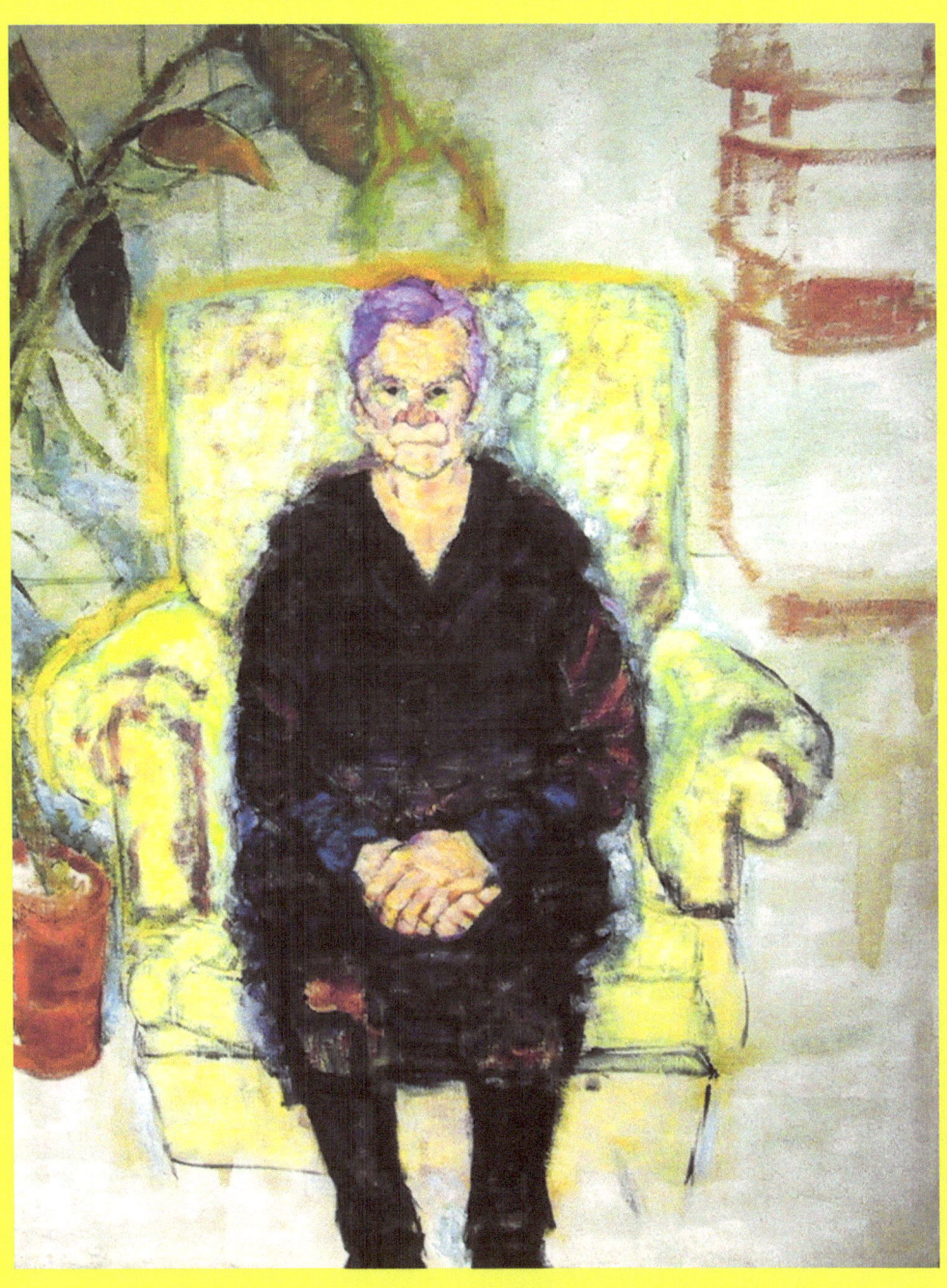

The pictures of places are called **landscapes.**

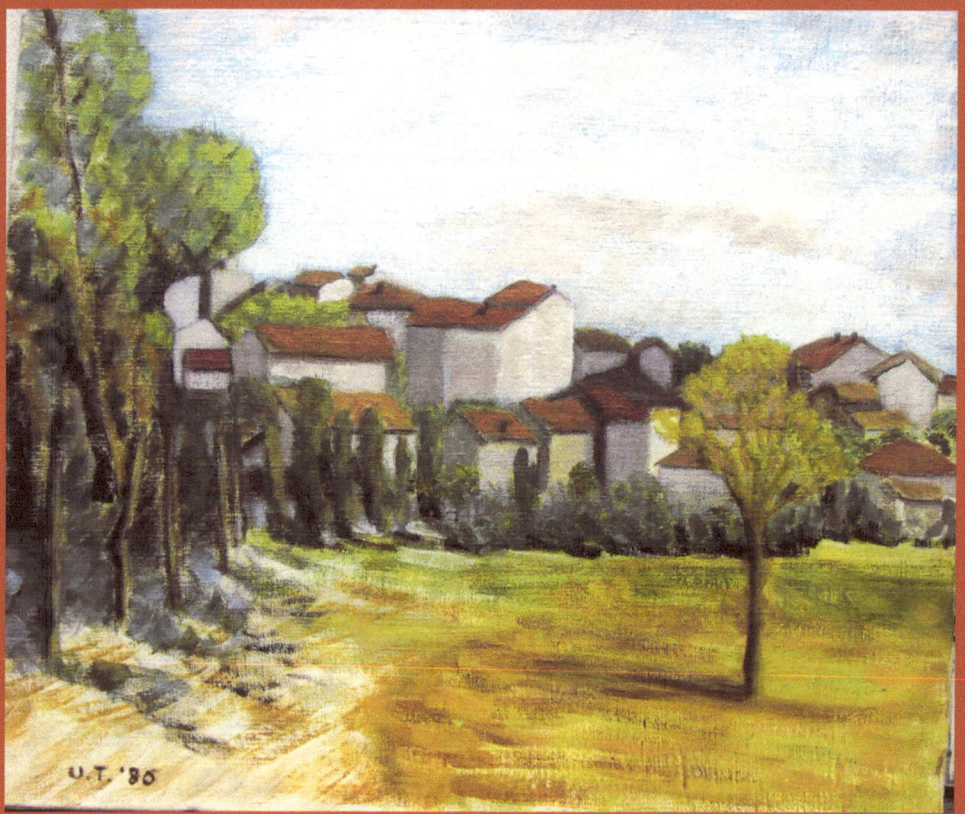

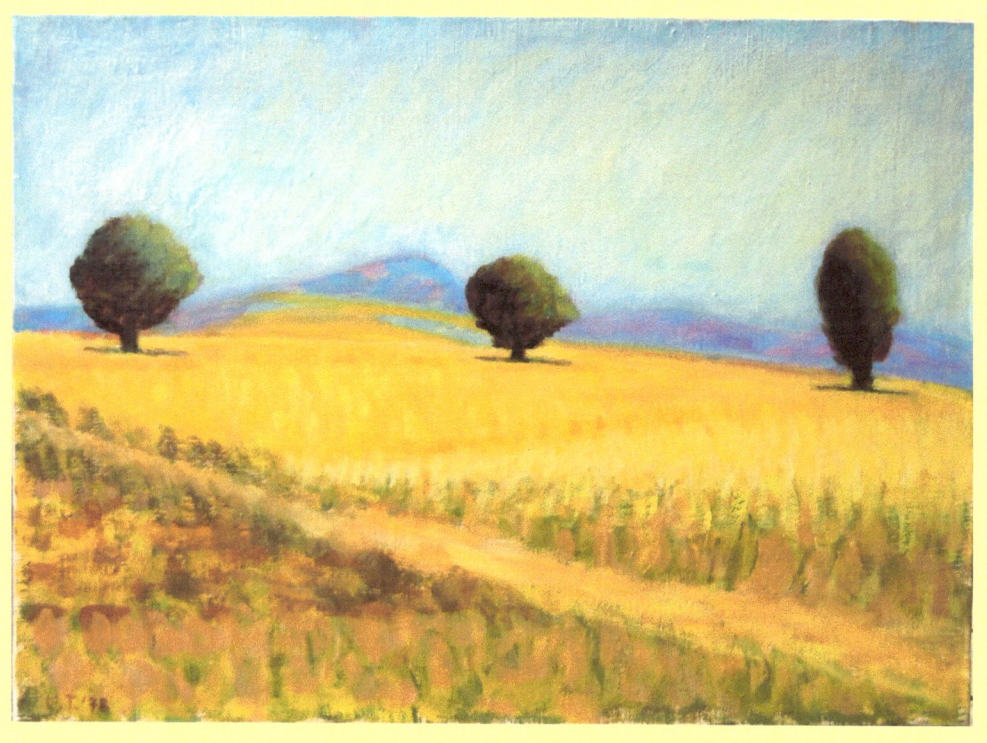

Ugo painted pictures of the countryside outside Rome.
Some pictures show trees and fields, some show buildings.

What do the pictures tell us about these places?

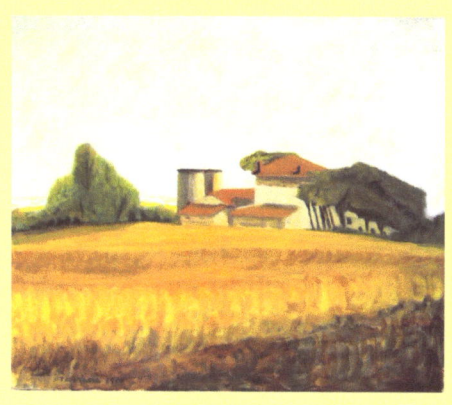

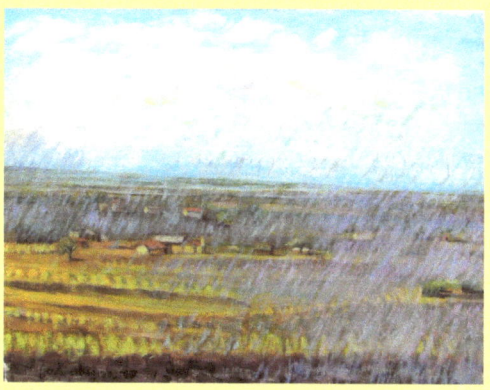

Some pictures show boats and the sea.

These pictures are called **seascapes.**

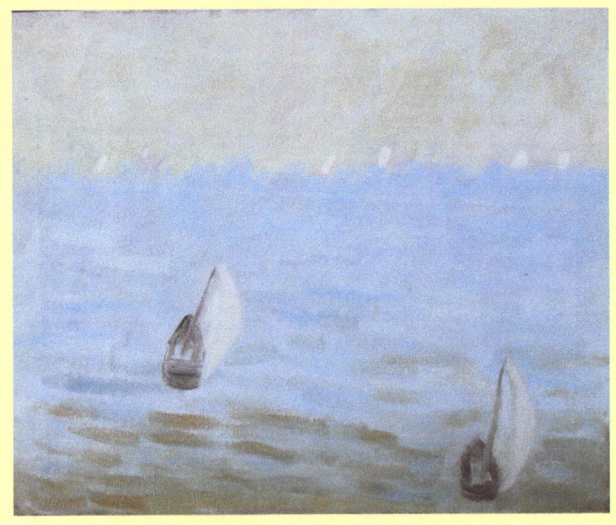

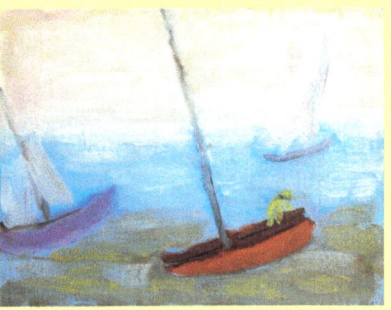

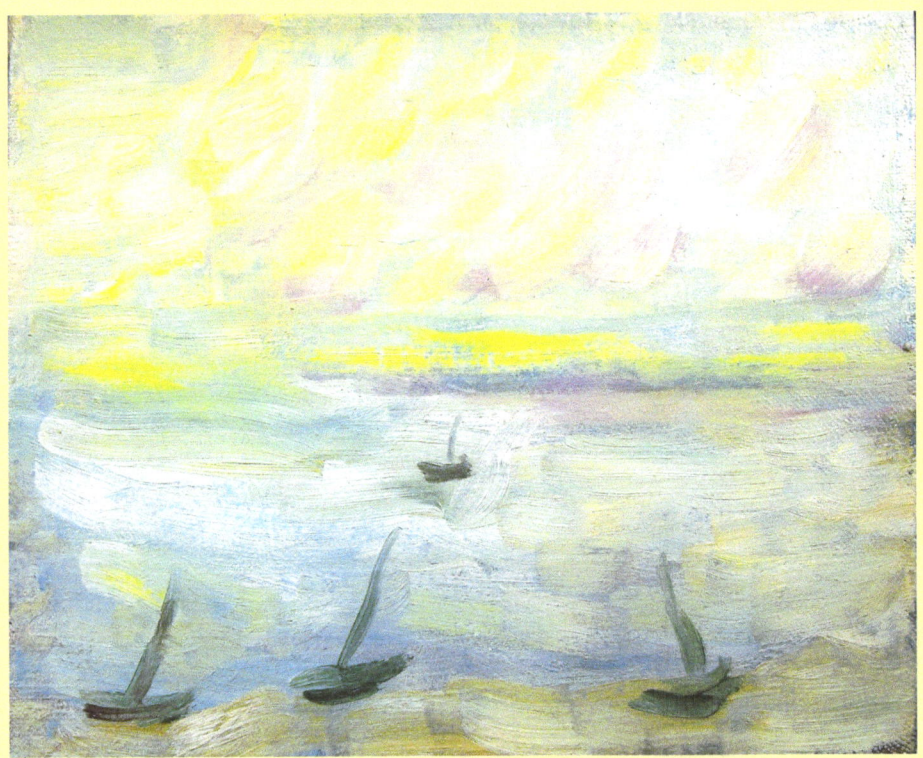

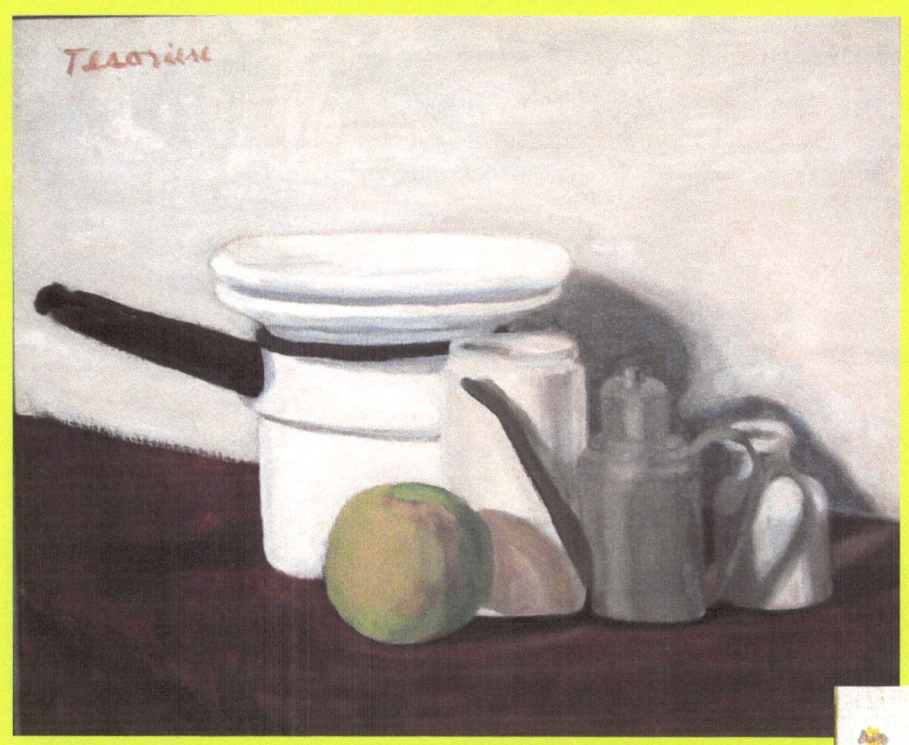

Pictures of things are called **_still life._**

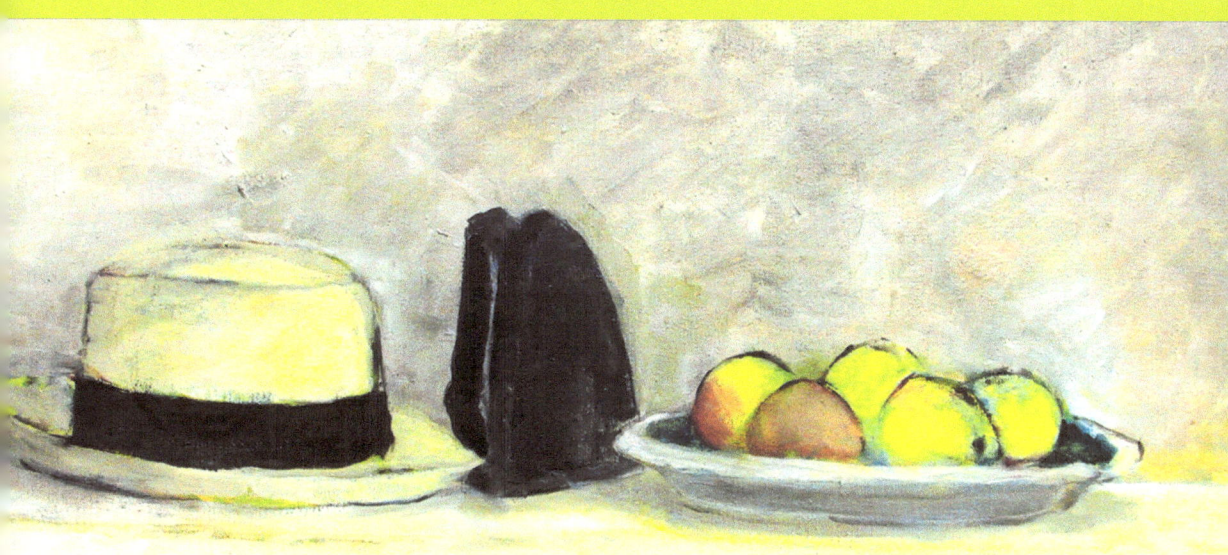

Ugo painted many objects that he had in his house and in his studio. Why do you think these pictures are called still life?

Do you have some of these objects in your home?

Pictures of people are called **portraits.**

They can show us how a person looks, and sometimes they can tell us what the person is like or what they do.

Let's look at some pictures of people and see what the artist is telling us.

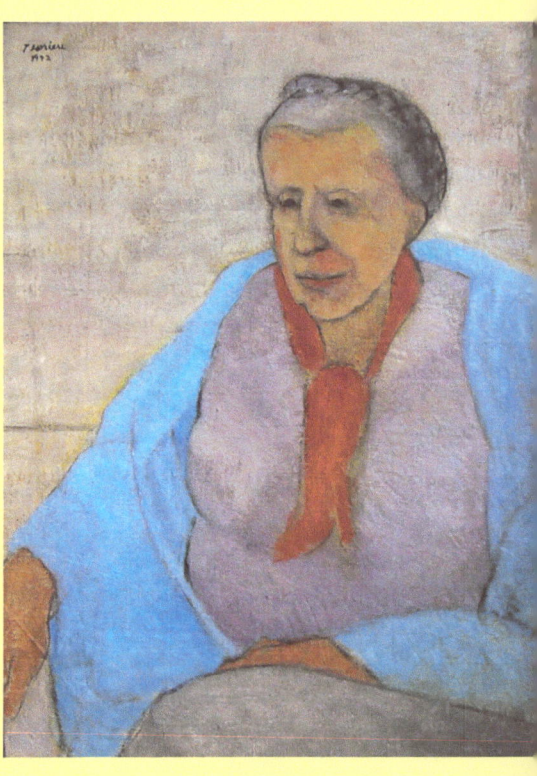

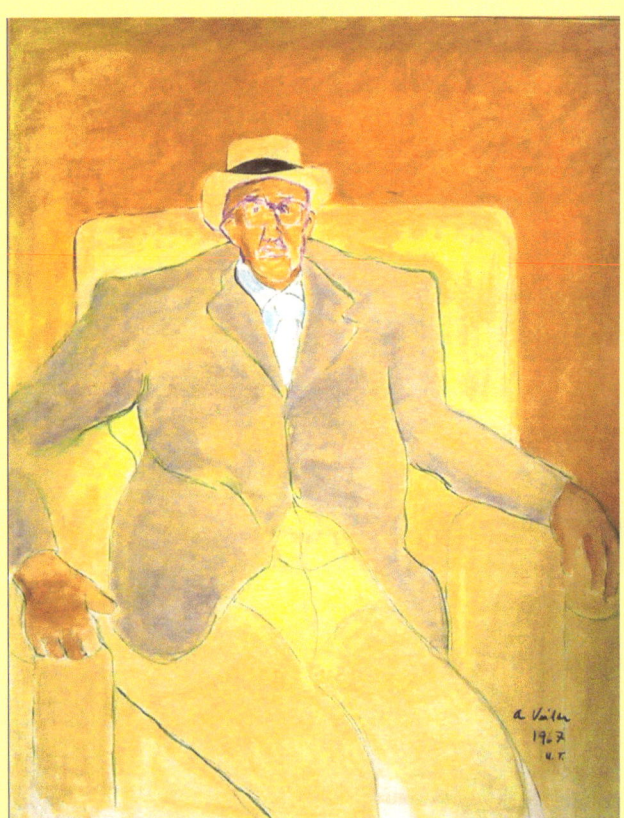

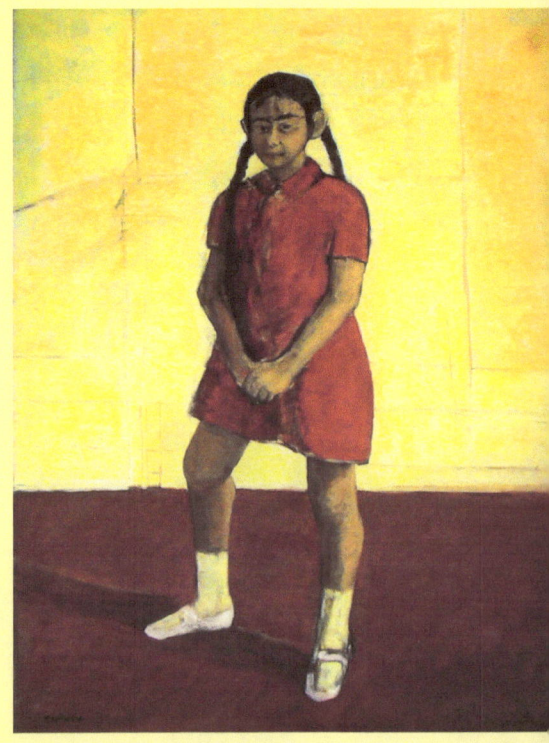

Look at all these portraits.

Can you tell which two pictures are of the same person?

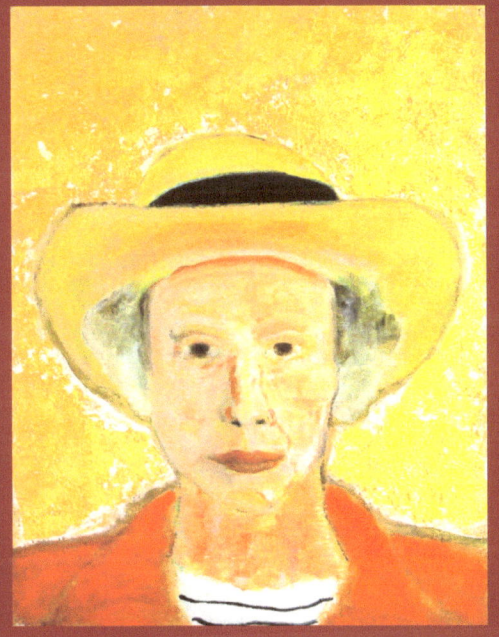

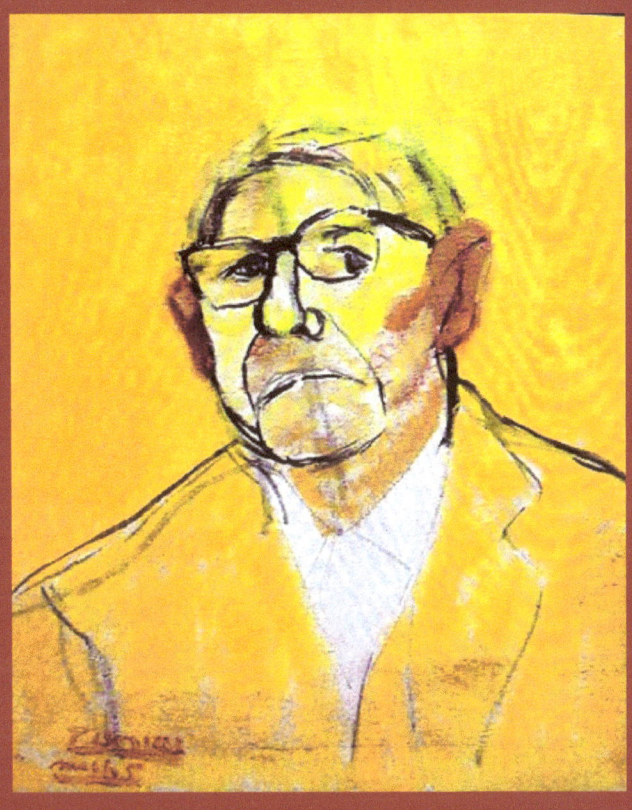

Since it's easier to take photographs of people to show what they look like, why do you think artists draw or paint portraits?

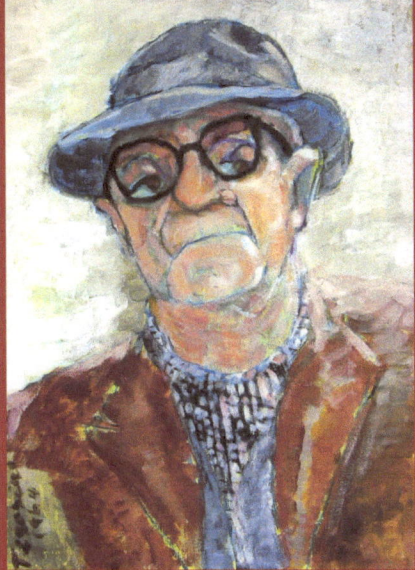

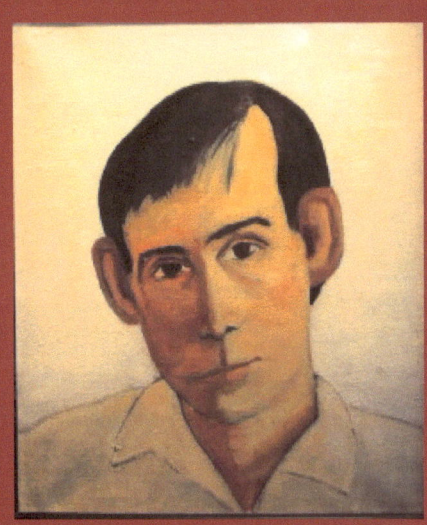

Sometimes an artist makes pictures of himself.

These pictures are called
self portraits

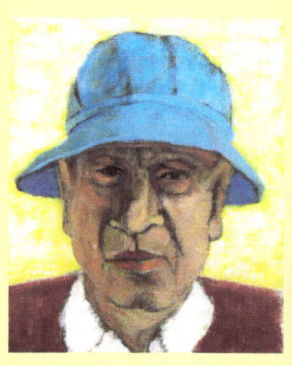

and often tell us a lot
about how the artists felt at
the time they were painted.
Ugo made all these pictures
of himself….. plus many,
many more!

Do you think Ugo looks
the same in these pictures
or different?

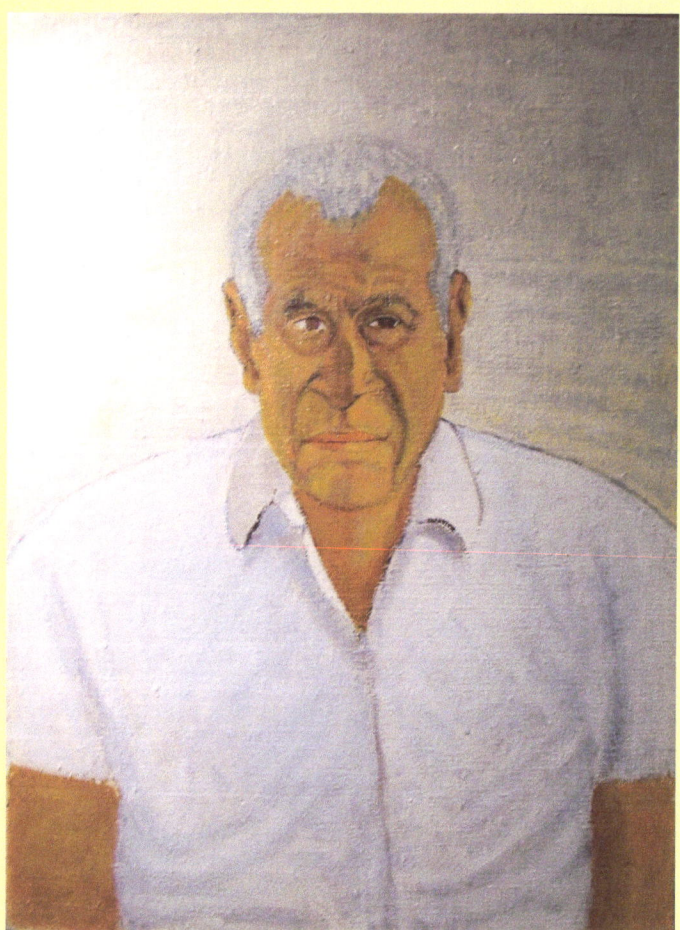

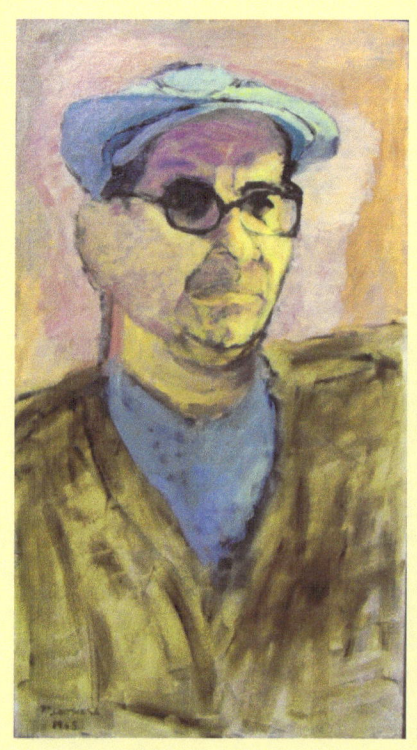

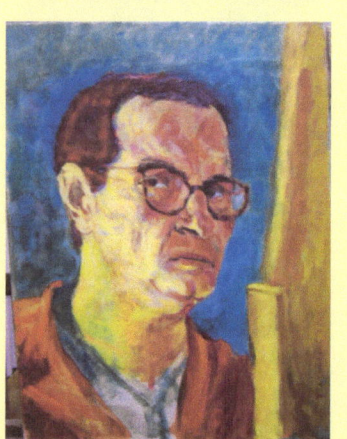

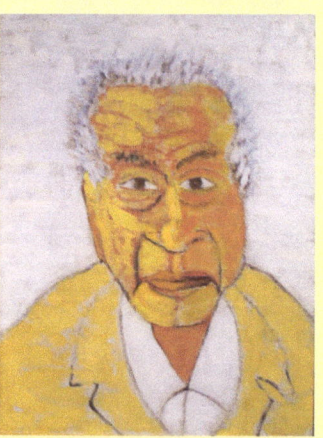

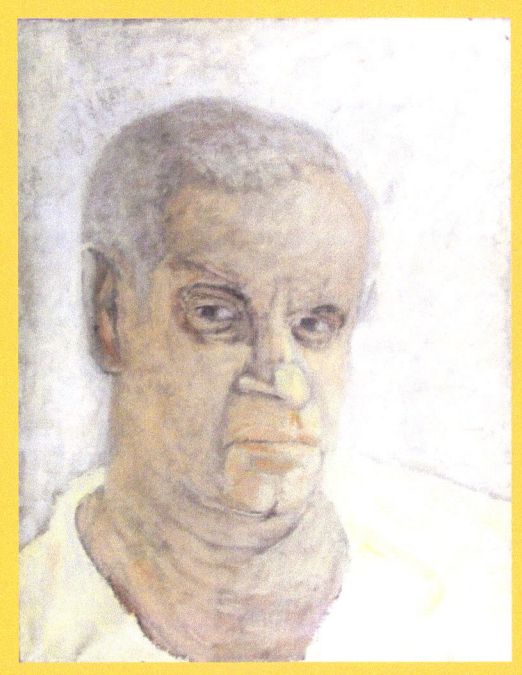

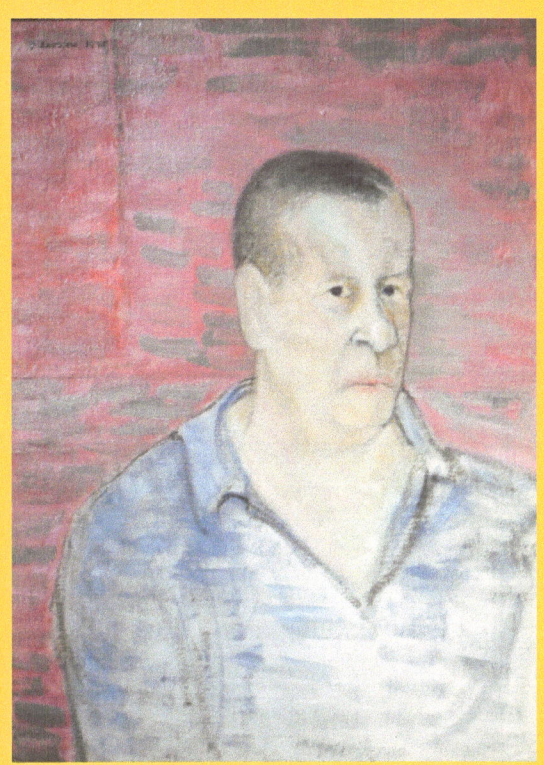

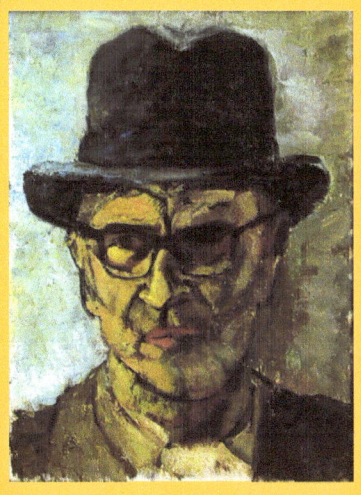

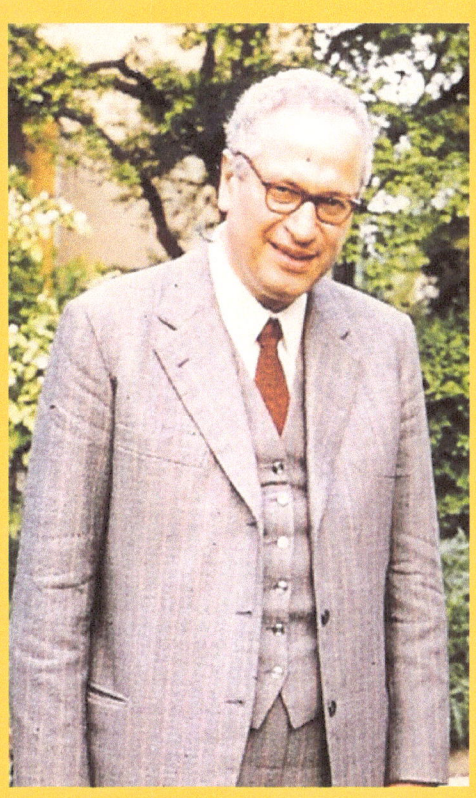

Here is a photograph of Ugo.

Do you think the pictures he made
of himself look like him?

Do you think it is important
that a self portrait looks like
the artist that made it?

Ugo studied at the Accademia and worked many years in his studio in Rome, learning a lot about artists and the pictures they made. Some of his favorite artisits were Cezanne, Picasso, Matisse and Morandi. Ugo learned something different by studying the work of each of these artists.

He learned about color from *Paul Cezanne*,

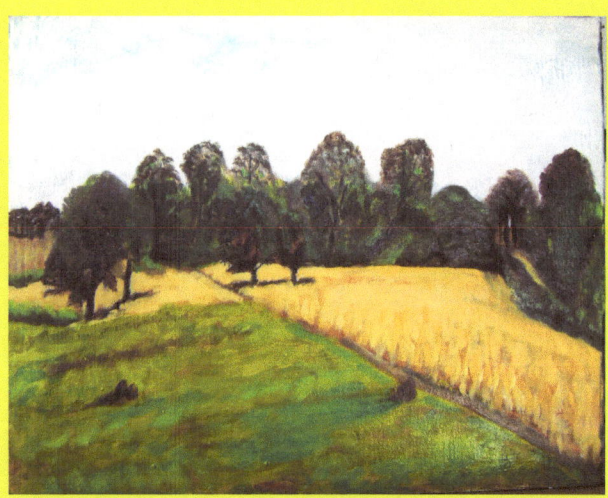

Ugo's picture

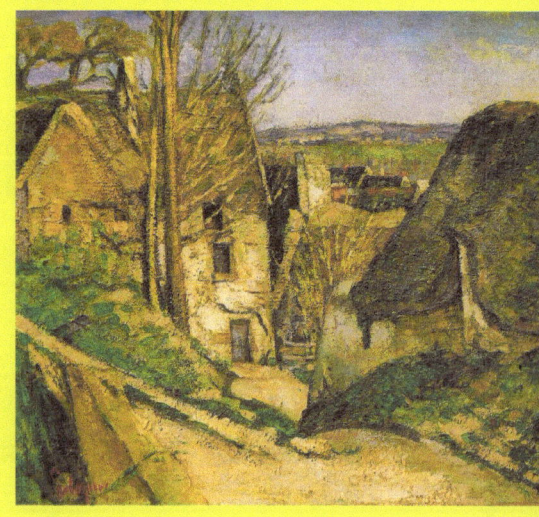

Cezanne's picture

and about still life from *Giorgio Morandi*.

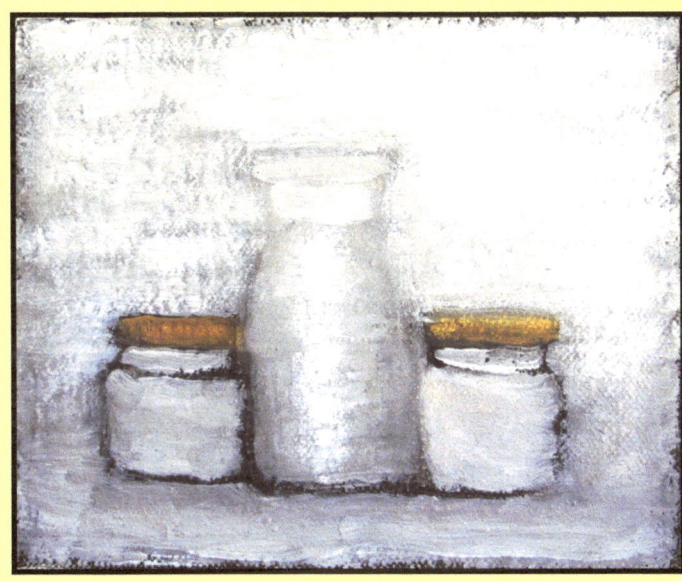

Ugo's picture

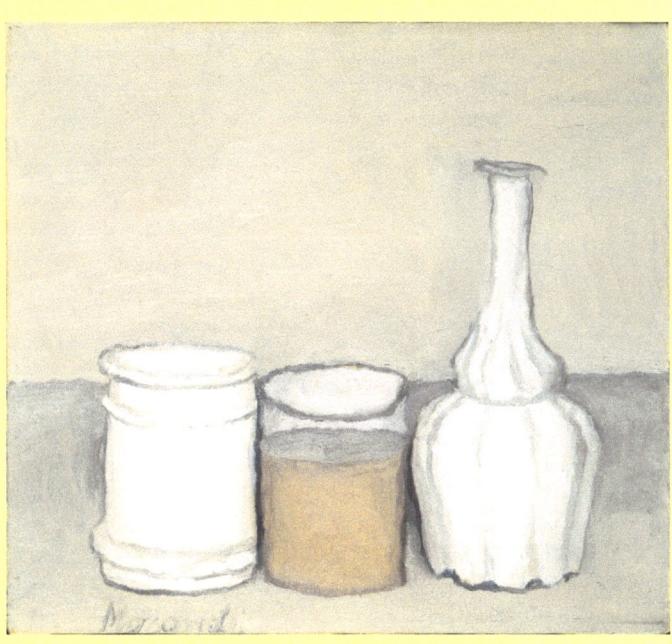

Morandi's picture

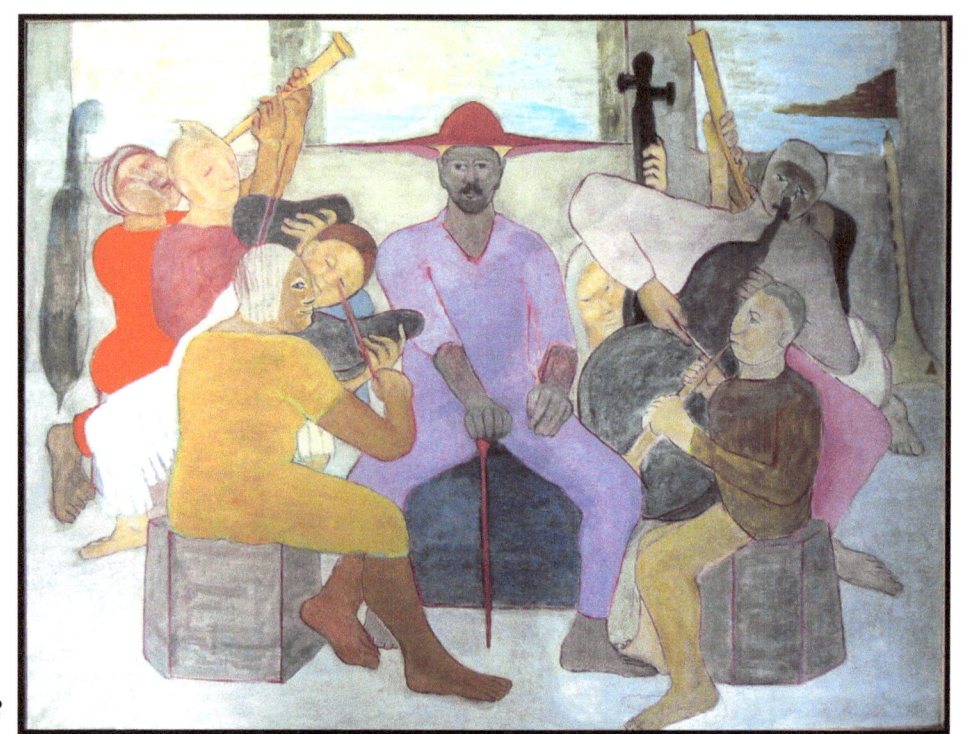

Ugo's picture

He learned about movement from **Pablo Picasso**,

Picasso's picture

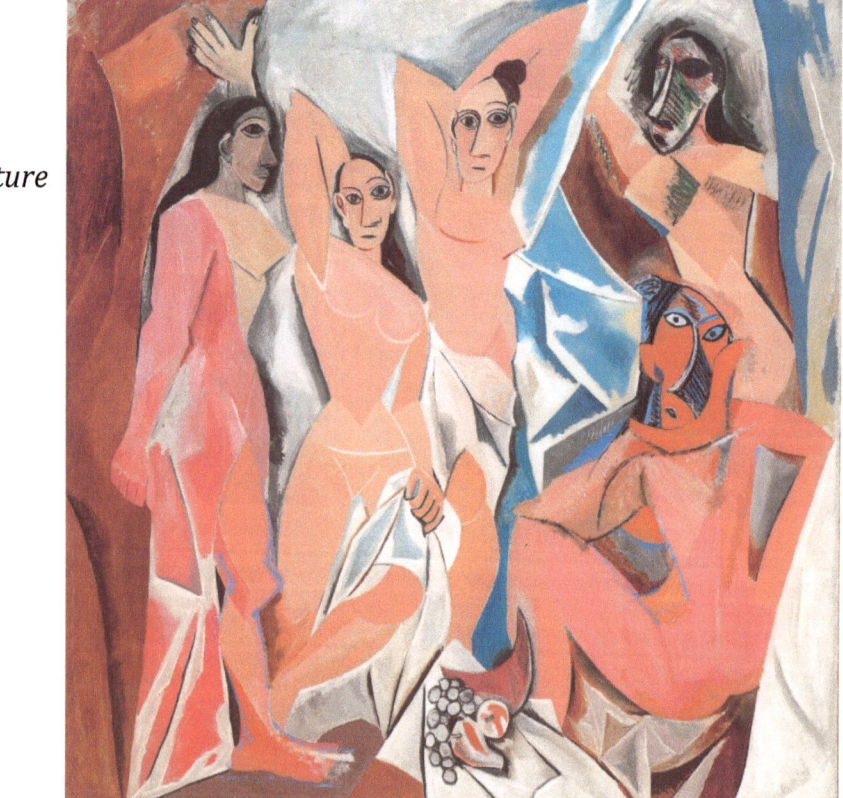

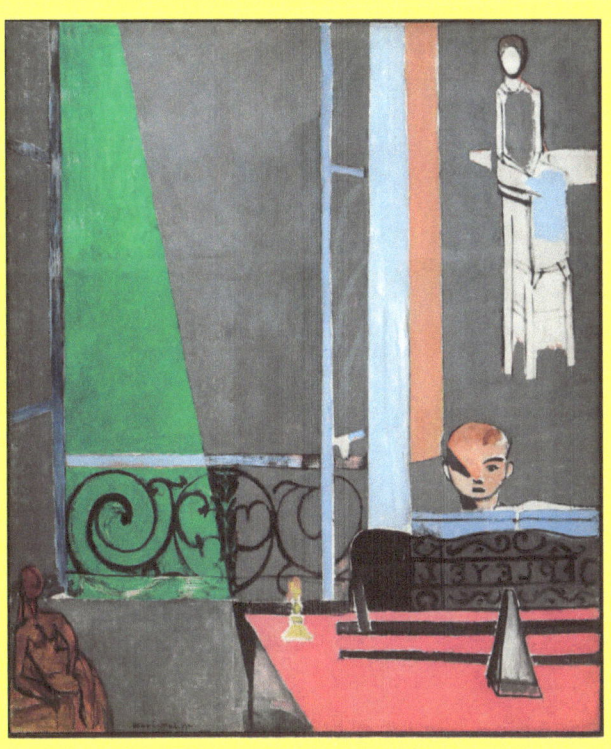

and about composition from *Henri Matisse.*

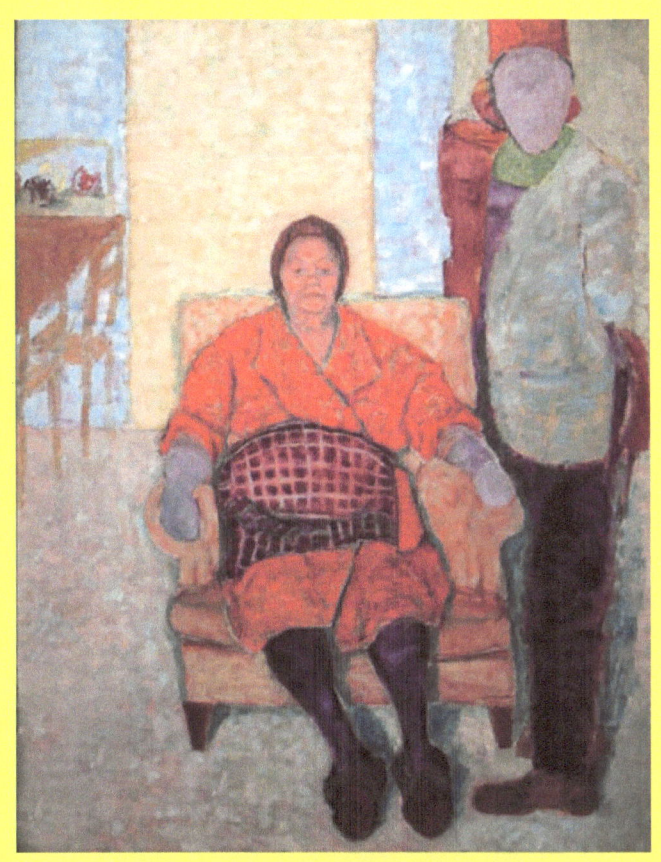

*Can you guess
which picture was
Ugo's?*

*The answer is on page 36

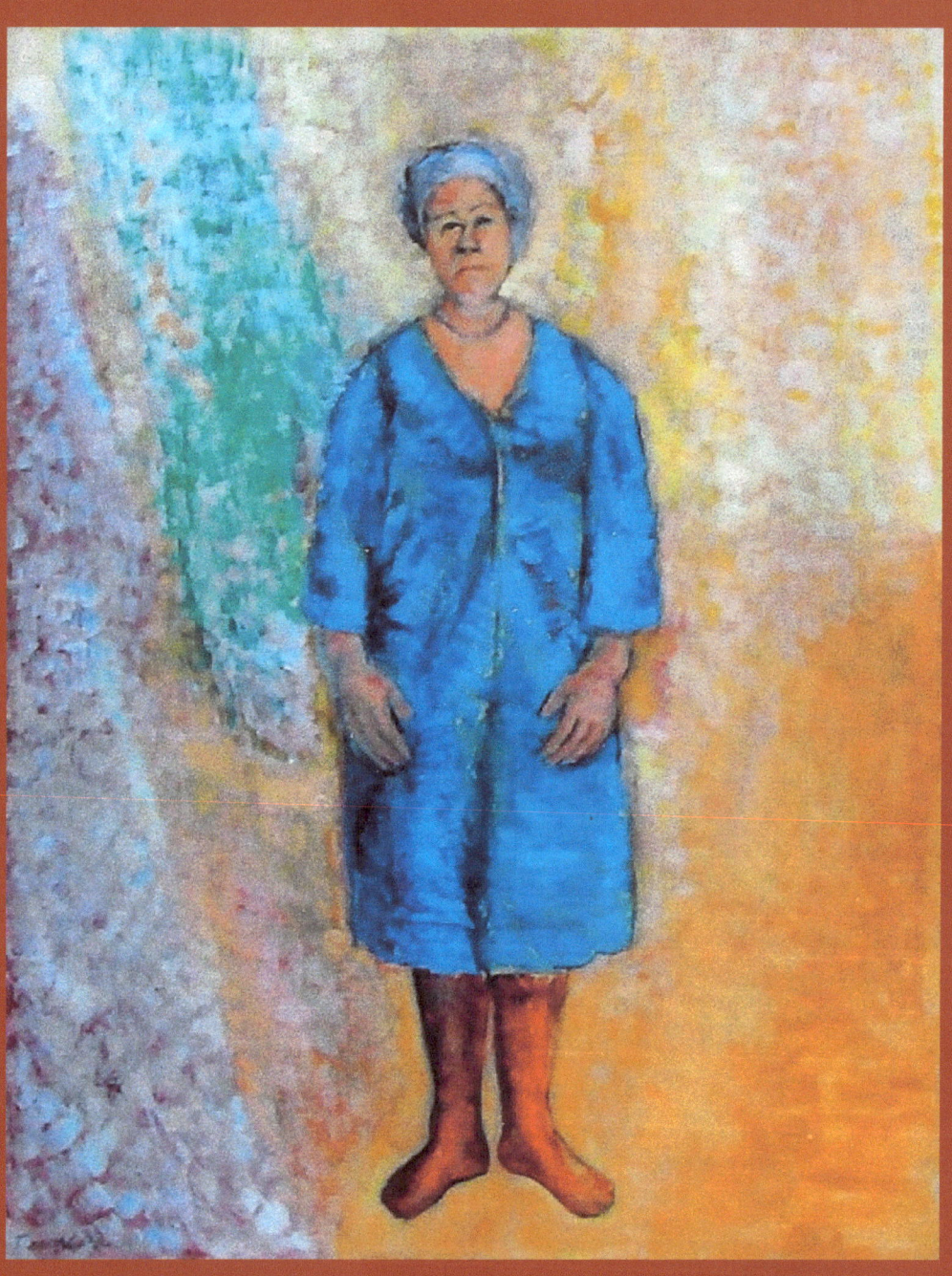

Just as Ugo learned from the many artists whose work he admired, he also learned from other people who were close to him.

His wife Valeria taught him about the work of one of her favorite artists named Giotto, and sometimes helped choose the people who sat for Ugo to have their portraits painted.

There was another friend of Ugo who helped him on his journey as an artist. His name was Francis. He was a young monk who was studying in Rome when they met.

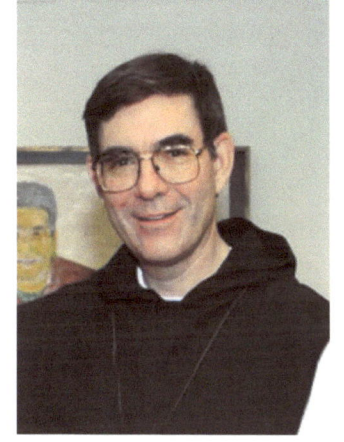

Ugo was an artist and Francis was a musician. They both agreed that making beautiful art and music was very important.

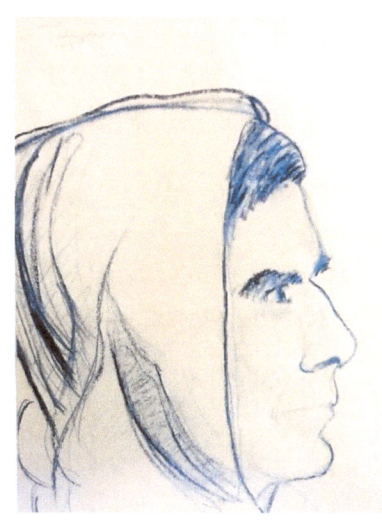

This is a picture Ugo made of Francis when he was a student in Rome.

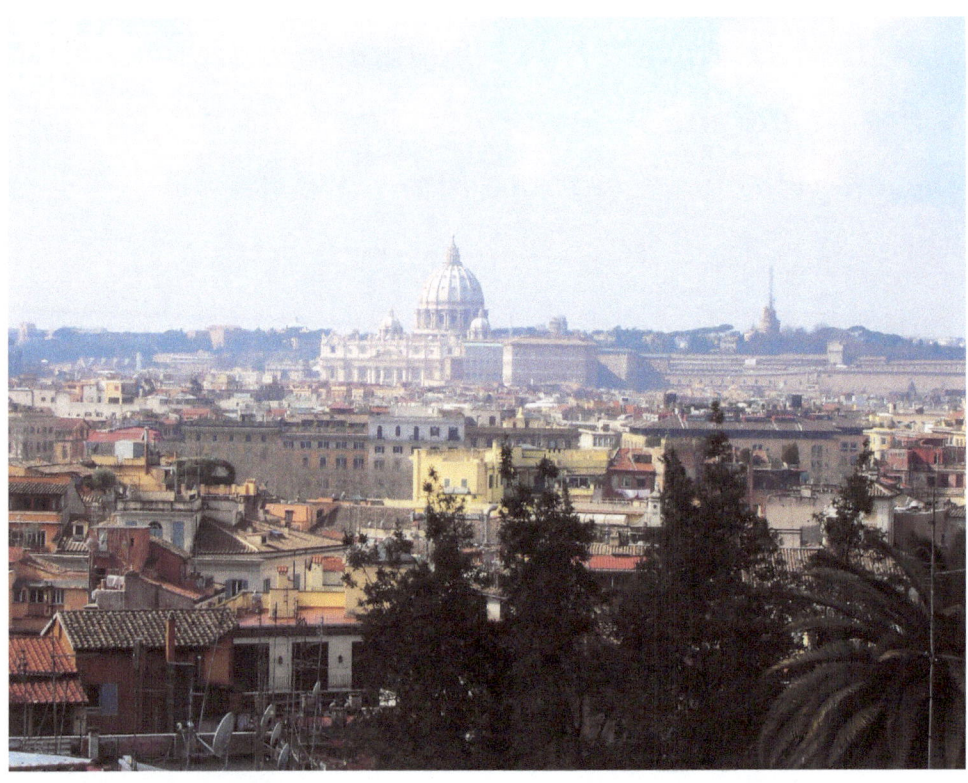

When they met, they became very best friends. Every week, Francis would visit Ugo and see the pictures he made since his last visit. Then they would go for a long walk around Rome. As they walked, Ugo would teach Francis everything he knew about art and Francis would share everything **he** was learning in school .

Then they would return home where Valeria had a delicious meal ready and they would all enjoy lunch together talking about art, life, and music.

Ugo, Valeria and Francis remained friends for many years, even after Francis left Rome and came home to the United States.

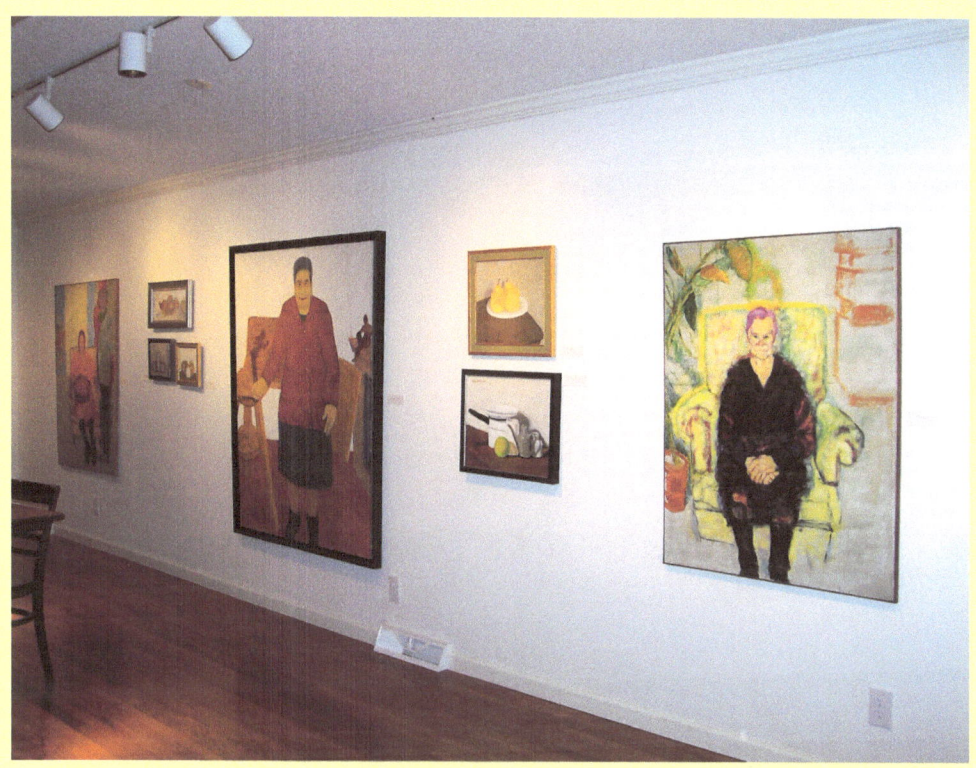

At the end of Ugo's life, he gave all his pictures to his friend Francis.

They are now in a Gallery at Francis's home, a monastery called Mepkin Abbey, near Charleston, South Carolina.

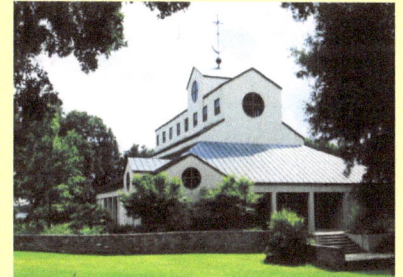

Just as Ugo learned from the many artists that came before him, we can learn a lot about art from Ugo's pictures...

...and if we look very carefully, we can also learn all about the man who made them.

Glossary and Pronunciation Guide

To **observe** is to look very carefully at something, paying attention to detail.

Ugo Tesoriere (**oo** go   teh soar ee **air** ee)* Born in 1923 in New York City, died in Rome, Italy in 2000

A visual artist is one who expresses himself in ways that can be observed by seeing, such as making pictures.

Leonardo Da Vinci (lee oh **nar** doe dah **vin** chee) Artist and inventor who lived from 1452 to1519 in Italy.

Michelangelo Buonarroti (mee kah **lahn** jello bow nah **roh** tee) Artist who lived from 1475 to 1564 in Italy.

The Sistine Chapel is in Vatican City, within Rome. Although it was built by Pope Sixtus IV in 1475, Pope Julius II was responsible for commissioning Michelangelo to paint the famous ceiling.

L' Accademia di Belle Arti, (lah cah **day** me ah dee **bell** ay **are** tay) translated as the academy of the beautiful arts, this is the most prestigious school of art in Rome.

Via Giulia (**vee** ah **jewel** yah) the street in Rome across the Tiber River from the Vatican, where the Tesorieres lived.

Composition refers to the visual structure of a picture.

A **monk** is a man who lives in a monastery, apart from the world and dedicates his life to prayer.

A **monastery** is a large building or group of buildings where monks live together in a life of prayer.

A **gallery** is a room or set of rooms where art is displayed.

Follow-Up Projects

* Set up a still life with three objects, then make a picture.
  Experiment by using different drawing materials or
  by rearranging the objects.

* Using a mirror, make a self portrait.

* Find a friend to work with and create portraits of each other.

* Make a portrait of someone in your family.
  Then, take a photograph of that person.
  Observe the differences in the two pictures.

* Make a portrait of your pet.

* Take your art supplies outside and make a picture
  of what you observe.

You can see more pictures that Ugo made by visiting
www.tesorierecollection.org

List of pictures and credits:

The artwork in this book was done by Ugo Tesoriere (1923-2000) and is part of the Tesoriere Collection at Mepkin Abbey unless otherwise noted

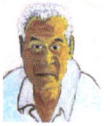
2000.1.005
Self Portrait
oil on canvas
50 x 70cm

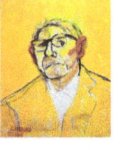
2000.1.006
Yellow Man
oil on canvas
47 x 39 cm

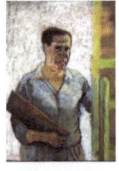
2000.1.005
Self Portrait
oil on canvas
50 x 70cm

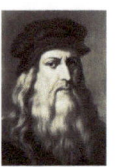
Leonardo DaVinci
Self Portrait

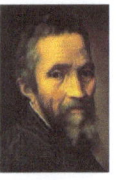
Michelangelo Buonaroti
Self Portrait
Casa Buonaroti, Florence, Italy

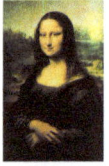
La Gioconda
By Leonardo DaVinci
oil on poplar panel
77 x 53 cm
Musee du Louvre, Paris, France

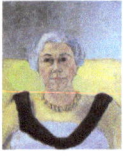
2000.1.016
Valeria with Nonna's Gold Necklace
oil on canvas
46 x 39 cm

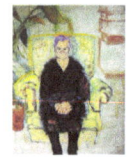
2000.1.020
Sor Michelina
oil on canvas
115 x 90 cm

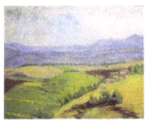
2000.1.153
Countryside Landscape
oil on canvas
70 x 90 cm

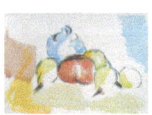
2000.2.0039
Still Life
watercolor on paper
21 x 31 cm

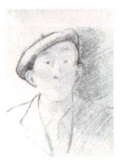
2000.2.0043
Lorenzo
pencil on paper
Collection of Barbara Burgess
And John Dinklespiel

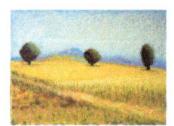
2000.2.060
The Three Trees
oil on canvas
49 x 70 cm

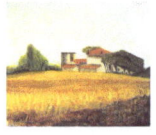
2000.1.036
Il Corneto
oil on canvas
55 x 64 cm

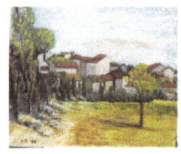
2000.1.065
Village Near Tolfa
oil on canvas
60 x 70 cm

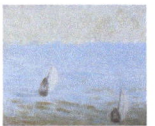
2000.1.191
Seascape
oil on canvas
40 x 50 cm

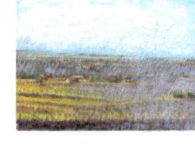
2000.1.135
April Showers
oil on canvas
58 x 78 cm
Collection of Mr and Mrs Ron Kline

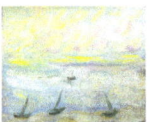
2000.1.172
Seascape with Sailboats
oil on canvas
20 x 25 cm
Collection of David & Wendy George

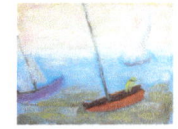
2000.1.066
Seascape with Red Sailboat
oil on canvas
15 x 20 cm

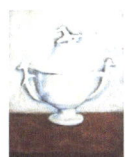

2000.1.263
Still Life with Sugar Bowl
oil on canvas
25 x 20 cm

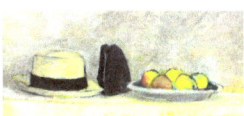

2000.1.046
Still Life with Hat & Iron
oil on canvas
34 x 73 cm

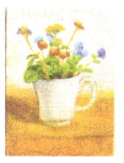

2000.1.126
Still Life with Flowers
oil on canvas
20 x 15 cm

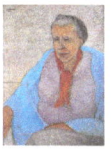

2000.1.021
Maria Teresa
oil on canvas
80 x 60 cm

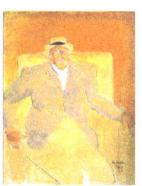

2000.1.028
A Visitor
oil on canvas
117 x 90 cm

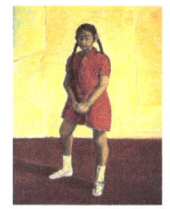

2000.1.02
"La Scugnizza"
oil on canvas
130 x 100 cm

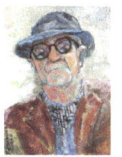

2000.1.007
Old Pensioner
oil on canvas
40 x 30 cm

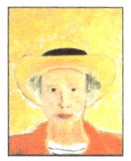

2000.1.244
Gina
oil on canvas
50 x 40 cm

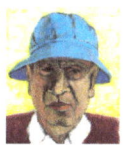

2000.1.013
Self Portrait
oil on canvas
30.5 x 25.5 cm

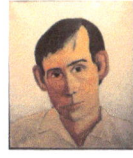

2000.1.027
Jeremy
oil on canvas
40 x 36 cm

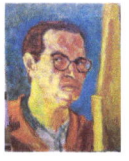

2000.1.382
Self Portrait
oil on canvas
50 x 40 cm

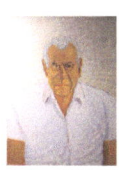

2000.1.137
Self Portrait
oil on canvas
85 x 65 cm

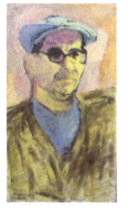

2000.1.121
The Sicilian
oil on canvas
70 x 40 cm

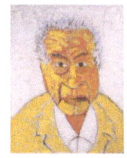

2000.1.014
Self Portrait
oil on canvas
50 x 40 cm

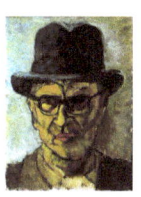

2000.1.012
Self Portrait with Opera Hat
oil on canvas
40 x 30 cm

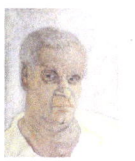

2000.1.192
Self Portrait
oil on canvas
50 x 40 cm

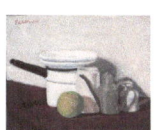

2000.1.052
White Pot with Green Apples
oil on canvas
40 x 50 cm

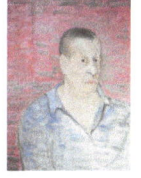

2000.1.275
Self Portrait
oil on canvas
80 x 60 cm

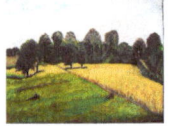

2000.1.270
Landscape
oil on canvas
34.5 x 45 cm
Collection of Mr and Mrs Mark Kline

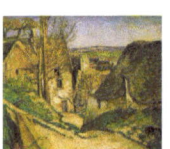

The House of the Hanged Man
Paul Cezanne (1839—1906)
Photo Credit: Erich Lessing /
Art Resource, NY

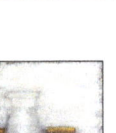

20001.042
Jars
oil on canvas
20 x 25 cm

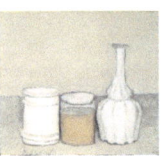

Still Life with Flask
Giorgio Morandi
© 2011 Artists Rights Society
(ARS),
New York / SIAE, Rome

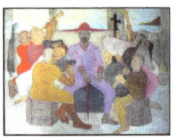

2000.1.285
Il Concerto
oil on canvas
200 x 150 cm
Collection of the Abbey of Gethsemani

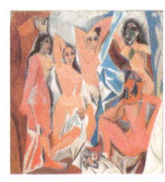

Les Demoiselles d'Avignon
Pablo Picasso (1881-1973)
oil on canvas
© 2011 Estate of Pablo Picasso,
Artists Rights Society (ARS),
New York

The Piano Lesson
Henri Matisse (1869-1954)
oil on canvas, 8'.5" x 6'11.75"
© 2011 Succession H. Matisse/
Artists Rights Society (ARS), New York

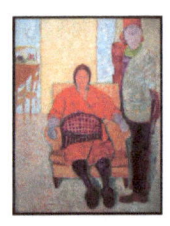

2000.1.018
Sor Marianina
oil on canvas
130 x 100 cm

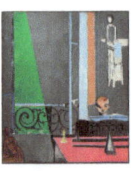

2000.1.364
Valeria with Red Stockings
oil on canvas
114 x 90 cm
Collection of Natalia De Micheli

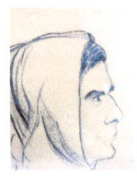

2000.2.0181
Francis
pencil on paper
28 x 22 cm
Collection of the author

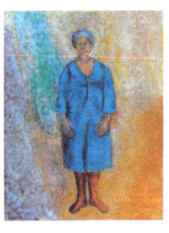

2000.1.008
Giovanna Standing
oil on canvas
150 x 120 cm

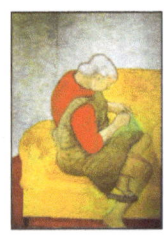

2000.1.001
Valeria Sewing
oil on canvas
140 x 100 cm

www.ingramcontent.com/pod-product-compliance
Lightning Source LLC
Chambersburg PA
CBHW050403180526
45159CB00005B/2135